DERBY
COUNTY
Football Club

1888 – 1996

DERBY COUNTY

Football Club

1888 – 1996

ANDY ELLIS

First published 2008

The History Press Ltd
The Mill, Brimscombe Port
Stroud, Gloucestershire, GL5 2QG
www.thehistorypress.co.uk

British Library Cataloguing in Publication Data.
A catalogue record for this book is available from the British Library.

ISBN 978 07524 4792 6

Typesetting and origination by The History Press Ltd.
Printed in Great Britain

Contents

About the Author

Andy Ellis has been a supporter of the Rams – initially at the Baseball Ground; now at Pride Park Stadium – since the age of seven when his father took him to stand on the Popside for a league match against Blackburn Rovers in March 1969.

His footballing travels thereafter have taken him all over England (and the occasional trip to Italy in the Anglo-Italian Cup) to watch his beloved club – from the humble surroundings of Halifax Town, Hartlepool United and York City to the imposing stadiums in Liverpool, Manchester and London.

A memorabilia collector of all things to do with Derby County – mainly post-war first-team programmes – Andy's first book, *Relics of the Rams* (Breedon Books, 2005), showcased many of the collectables, ephemera and trophies associated with Derby County – not only those on public display in trophy cabinets but also in the various storerooms within Pride Park and, more importantly, in various private collections around the country.

Andy works as a business intelligence consultant and lives in the city with his wife Jenny and two daughters, Naomi and Katie.

Acknowledgements

Many books have been published over the last twenty years covering every aspect of life in and around Derby County Football Club. These previous works include various versions of the *Complete Record* and *Who's Who*; *The Derby County Story* and a recent trend of ex-player biographies from Charlie George, Archie Gemmill, Peter Shilton, Colin Todd, Dave Mackay and Brian Clough.

As the club enters its 125th year, one hopes that this photographic record pulls together some famous faces, teams and images from the first 108 years of league football and brings back memories of those lucky enough to have seen some of them play.

Many of these photographs are seen for the first time in this book and I would like to thank the following for their support and help, either with information and advice, loan of pictures or the permission for their use: Derby County Football Club; Garth Jones; Gerald Mortimer, for team line-ups and statistics from his previous works; Steve Pocock; Joe Stack of W.W. Winter Ltd; Ian Stals and Nick Tomlinson at www.picturethepast.org. One must not forget Tom Glick and Roger Faulkner, directors of Derby County, who each took time out to write a foreword.

Last, but by no means least, Stephen Holford at the History Press for making this photographic record a reality.

Foreword

By Roger Faulkner

Andy Ellis's remarkable photographic history of Derby County comes at a very appropriate time as we approach the 125th anniversary of the founding of the club. It is a mellowing thought to realise that I have been a supporter of the club for more than half that time. In his wonderful book *Fever Pitch*, Nick Hornby relates how the major milestones of his life were inextricably tied in his memory to the Arsenal results at the time. While that may seem extreme, I can empathise with his thinking. In my own case, my baptism as a lifelong Rams' supporter came on 27 April 1946. My father had just returned from the war and I knew neither him nor what a holiday was. As we huddled around a small wooden radio in the Chimes Hotel, Bournemouth, listening to the FA Cup final, I believe I bonded with him and Derby County at the very same moment.

There are so many memories since that time as I followed the team's tortuous journey down to the old Third Division North to the improbable glories of First Division titles and European competition under Brian Clough, Peter Taylor and Dave Mackay. The roller-coaster ride continued, taking me vicariously to the High Court in the 1980s when the club was in peril, back to Premiership respectability under Jim Smith and then on to that incredible day at Wembley just a year ago.

Thank you Derby County for adding so much to my life and, on behalf of all Derby County supporters, thank you Andy Ellis, for capturing so much of the rich history of the club in this wonderful book.

Roger Faulkner
Non-Executive Director, Derby County
Michigan, May 2008

Foreword

By Tom Glick

One of the first things that impressed me about Derby County was the rich history and heritage of the club. As a newcomer, I was determined to learn it rapidly and well. On an early flight from the States, I tore through Andy Ellis' first book from cover to cover and finished it feeling enriched, well informed and wanting to learn more. Thank goodness for this, his latest publication, which has deepened my understanding and passion for this great club.

Since joining Derby County a few months ago, I have been overwhelmed by the quality of the support the club enjoys. In fact, the resilient and unwavering Derby County supporters have been well documented in the national media during this past season, filling Pride Park match after match during some very trying times on the pitch. Families throughout Derbyshire, and indeed now worldwide, pass the tradition of their support for the Rams from generation to generation. This devotion needs to be continually encouraged and fed so that young supporters can learn about the great moments, players and managers from the last 125 years and so that lifelong fans can relive their favourite Rams memories. We, as the club's ownership and management, are committed to this, and we are grateful that Andy Ellis dedicates his time, talent and passion to this great cause. Enjoy the book!

Tom Glick
President & Chief Executive, Derby County
June 2008

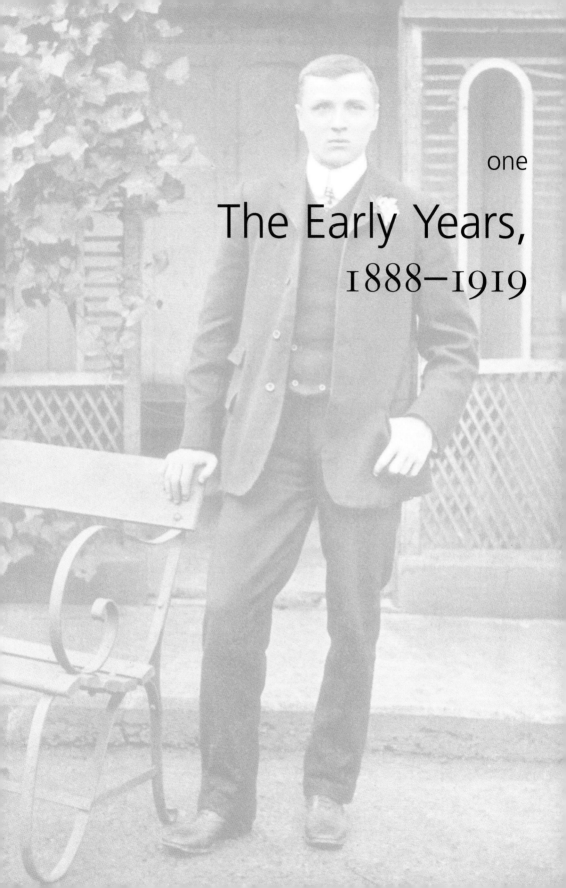

one

The Early Years, 1888–1919

Above: The Derby County team pictured on the steps of the football pavilion prior to their first home league game against West Bromwich Albion on 15 September 1888. They are wearing the original cricket club colours of blue, amber and chocolate. They lost this historic match 2-1, with Henry Plackett scoring in front of an approximate attendance of 3,000. Back row, left to right: William Morley (chairman), Marshall, Dakin (trainer), Latham, William Chatterton (reserve), Monks, Ferguson, Roulstone. Front row: Williamson, Bakewell, Cooper, Higgins, H. Plackett, L. Plackett.

John Goodall was one of the most famous players of his era – an England international and member of the famous Preston 'Invincibles' team. He signed for Derby in May 1889 and is credited with mentoring Steve Bloomer while they were at the club together. In all, he made 238 appearances, scoring 85 goals in his nine years with Derby, and was the first Rams player to captain England.

Opposite bottom: The Rams squad for the 1889/90 season. Back row right to left: W. Chatterton, A. Williamson, A. Latham, A. Goodall, Dakin (trainer), A. Ferguson, W. Roulstone, Bulmer (umpire). Front row: G. Bakewell, A. Higgins, J. Goodall, S. Holmes, L. Cooper, R. Milarvie.

   Chatterton also had the distinction of playing Test cricket for England and also played in Derby's first ever FA Cup game, as well as having played during the inaugural first league season. Also pictured are Bakewell, who scored two of the goals in Derby's first league game at Bolton, and Higgins, who scored four goals on his international debut for Scotland but was never selected again.

The Baseball Ground was created by Sir Francis Ley on a playing field used for his workers. The game of baseball was brought to England by Sir Francis and the Derby club was the first to be established. Steve Bloomer later played for the club and they became English champions in 1890. The Derby team pictured is, left to right, T. Presbury, E. Booth, D. Allsopp, J.P. Reidenbach, Sir Francis Ley, W.C. Bryan, S.D. Bullas, H.M. Middleton, W. North and J. Mellows

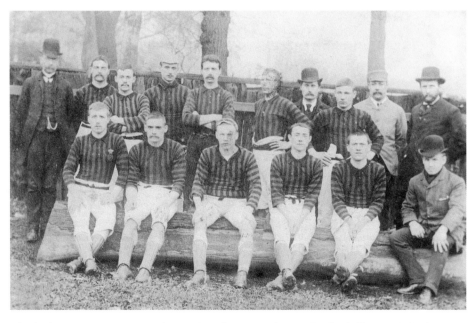

The Derby Junction team, 1891. At one time there were three major football teams in Derby – Derby County, Derby Midland and Derby Junction (formed from the old boys of Junction Street school). Derby Midland were swallowed up by Derby County and Derby Junction folded after a couple of seasons in the Midland League, though not before they reached the semi-finals of the FA Cup in 1890.

Preston North End *v*. Derby, 'A Goal'. An undated postcard, probably from the early 1900s, depicting the crowd celebrating at Deepdale, Preston.

Archie Goodall arrived at Derby from Aston Villa to join his elder brother John. Owing to their father's job in the army, they were born in different countries. Therefore, John turned out for England, while Archie played for Northern Ireland. Archie's career for the Rams lasted fourteen years and 423 appearances before he moved to Plymouth Argyle in 1903. After finishing his playing career, he became a renowned strongman act and travelled across Europe and the USA.

The FA Cup final against Sheffield United, 15 April 1899. An impressive set of results – 6-0 at Woolwich Arsenal; 2-1 *v.* Wolves; 2-1 *v.* Southampton; 3-1 *v.* Stoke – saw Derby reach a second successive final at Crystal Palace, having lost to rivals Nottingham Forest 3-1 the year before. The match ball from the game is on display in the Sheffield United Hall of Fame.

A very heavy pitch and a second-half injury to Johnny May, coupled with the suspension of the experienced Archie Goodall, saw the Rams' 1-0 half-time lead turn into a 4-1 defeat. In the background, the outline of the huge Crystal Palace arena can be seen. Derby's team that day was: Fryer, Methven, Staley, Cox, Paterson, May, Arkesden, Bloomer, Boag, McDonald and Allen. The attendance at the match was an impressive 73,833.

The 1899 FA Cup final ticket and programme. The original price on the ticket is 5s, which equates to £20 today, and the 1d programme would now be 32 pence. As an interesting comparison, an 1899 Derby County season ticket cost 12s 6d, approximately £50 today.

Both of these items are extremely rare and the programme would be worth several thousands of pounds at auction.

Steve Bloomer poses in a relaxed manner away from the football field in 1900. He was to have two spells with the Rams, joining Middlesbrough for a four-year spell in 1906.

In September 2008 Bloomer was inducted into the National Football Museum Hall of Fame.

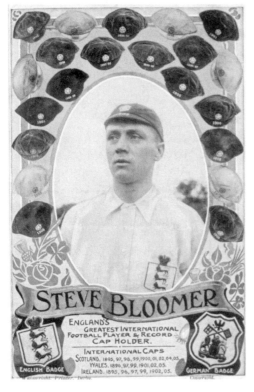

By 1900 Bloomer had become the highest-paid player on the staff, taking home £5 per week during the summer and winter. The average wage for other players was around £3. He also played baseball for the successful Derby club of the 1890s.

Described as the finest inside-right forward of all time, Steve Bloomer said of his mentor John Goodall: 'He was a fine teacher.' After moving to Derby County, he began playing for a team called Derby Swifts and was soon signed by the Rams on a wage of 7s 6d per week and made his debut against Stoke on 3 September 1892. He went on to score 352 goals for the club.

During the First World War, Bloomer was interned at Ruhleben, a civilian detention camp. In 1914, Bloomer went to Germany to coach the Berlin Britannia football club. Just three weeks later, war was declared and he found himself in the civilian prison camp at Ruhleben until March 1918, when he was released into Holland, although it was not until November when arrived back in England.

After the war he was a coach, both abroad and with the Derby reserves, a newspaper columnist and a groundsman at the Baseball Ground. The highlight of his coaching career came in 1924, when he guided Real Unión to victory in the Copa del Rey in Spain. Derby also paid for him to go on a cruise to Australia and New Zealand. He died three weeks after returning in April 1938 and his grave can been seen in the Nottingham Road Cemetery.

The text on this postcard of Bloomer says: 'He was born at Cradley Heath, near Birmingham, in 1874, and stands 5ft 7in in height. He has had a surfeit of international honours, due to his great speed, fine judgment and magnificent shooting at goal. He is an inside-right forward that Scottish players dread.'

Ben Warren was known for his hard but fair tackling, as well as for his consistent performances. He scored eight goals in seven FA Cup matches to help Derby reach the semi-finals of the competition in 1902. He was also one of England's highest-rated half-backs, winning his first international cap against Ireland in 1906. He made 242 league appearances for Derby, scoring 19 goals. A serious knee injury while playing for Chelsea meant that he would face a long lay-off and he suffered a mental breakdown as a result. By 1912 he had been admitted to the Pastures lunatic asylum in Mickleover and later died of tuberculosis while still an inmate in 1917.

In front of a crowd of 40,500, the Rams defence holds firm against a Millwall attack in the FA Cup semi-final at Villa Park on 21 March 1903. Derby won comfortably 3-0, with goals from Warren, Boag and Richards. Derby's team that day was: Fryer, Methven, Morris, Warren, A. Goodall, May, Warrington, York, Boag, Richards and Davis.

Bloomer receives the ball from a throw-in by John Boag during the 1904/05 season. Unfortunately no further information of the opposition is available.

The Derby County squad for 1903/04. Back row, left to right: A. Latham (trainer), B. Warren, J. Methven, B. Hall, W.H. Sargent (assistant secretary), H. Maskery, C. Morris, J. May, H.J. Newbould (secretary-manager), J.T. Mercer, S. Bloomer (captain), G. Davis, C. Leckie, J. Hodgkinson, G.R.H. Richards, J. Warrington.

This team finished fourteenth in the First Division and escaped relegation by two points. They also reached the FA Cup semi-finals, losing 1-0 to Bolton Wanderers.

Match action from a 1904 league encounter against rivals Nottingham Forest at the City Ground.

Right: This postcard from the *Kentish Independent* was produced for the Woolwich Arsenal *v.* Derby match on 18 March 1905; the game finished 0-0. The comment on the card reads: 'Oh I say … Now I've got you here I'm blessed if my knife is sharp enough to do the job decent, like. You'd better go home and come back again when I've got it sharpened.'

Below: The Popside (then known as the Railway Terrace) crowd for the FA Cup match against Newcastle United that ended as a 0-0 draw on 3 February 1905. The attendance was given as 18,000. Two observations of this picture are the lack of any female spectators and almost everyone is wearing a flat-cap – football was a game for the working man.

"KENTISH INDEPENDENT" FOOTBALL CARTOON.
(Reproduced by kind permission of the Proprietors).

DERBY COUNTY
v.
WOOLWICH ARSENAL.
MARCH 18th, 1905.
Result: Arsenal 0, Derby County 0.

REDSHIRT: Oh, I say. Now I've got you here I'm blessed if my knife is sharp enough to do the job decent like. You'd better go home and come again when I've got it sharpened.
"Molyneux" Series, No. 30

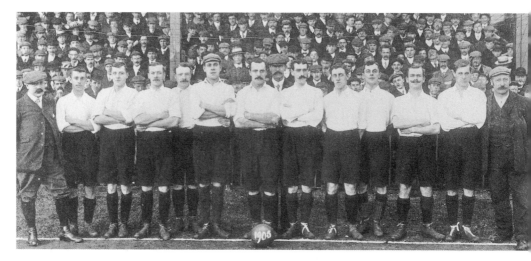

The Derby County squad for the 1905/06 season. Left to right: H. Newbould (secretary-manager), J. Davis, S. Bloomer, B. Warren, J. Methven, H. Maskery, C. Morris, W. Sargeant (assistant-secretary), T. Paton, B. Hall, G. Richards, F. Middleton, A. Wood.

That season, Bloomer was sold to Middlesbrough and manager Harry Newbould left in July 1906 to take over at Manchester City in protest.

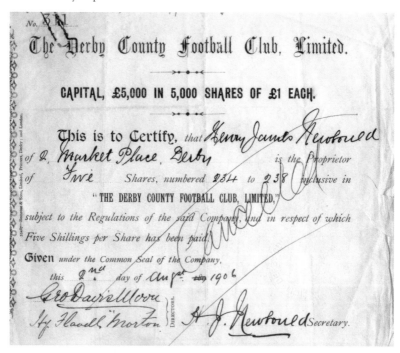

Harry Newbould was a qualified accountant and took the title of secretary-manager to begin with and basically ran all facets of the club. He is recognised as the club's first real manager in dealing with footballing matters and was responsible for bringing many famous players to the Rams. His share certificate, in his full name of Henry James Newbould, is signed by himself and gives his address as 2 Market Place, Derby. Interestingly it is dated as August 1906, a month after he had moved to Manchester City as manager.

The 1906/07 Rams squad who were relegated for the first time in the club's history. They are, back row, left to right: J. Nicholas, H. Maskery, C. Morris, Arthur Latham (trainer). Middle row: J. Methven (player-manager), F. Cleaver, B. Warren, B. Hall, A. Wood, W.S. Moore (secretary), unknown. Front row: J. Davis, J. Wood, J. Long, G. Richards, G. Davis. The newly appointed manager made the last five appearances of his playing career during this season.

The 1910/11 squad pose after training at the Baseball Ground. Back row, left to right: Jimmy Methven (manager), R. Frith, J. Nicholas, G. Lawrence, J. Atkin, J. Bauchop, G. Richards, A. Latham (trainer). Middle row: R. Lyle, H. Barnes, J. Bagshaw, E. Garry, W. Halligan, D. Donald, mascot. Front row: W. Grimes, B. Hall, A. Bentley, T. Barbour.

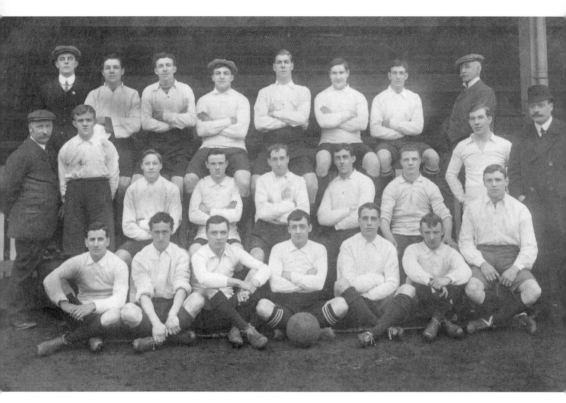

The Derby squad photographed after the return of Bloomer during the 1910/11 season (front row, third from the left). Bloomer returned to Derby from Middlesbrough to the delight of Rams fans at the age of thirty-five and, on his first match back at the Baseball Ground, doubled the attendance from the previous home game.

two

Between the Wars,
1920–39

The Derby County team before the 1-1 draw against West Bromwich Albion at the Baseball Ground, 25 September 1920. Back row, left to right: H. Wightman, J. Atkin, G. Lawrence, A. Ritchie, B. McLaverty. Front row: G. Thornewell, J. Moore, J. Lyons, F. Waterhouse, W. Murray, A. Quantrill. The picture is taken at the Normanton End, facing the original main stand with the terraced houses behind.

An aerial photogrpah of the Leys foundry also showing the Baseball Ground in 1921. The old pavilion building can still be seen, as can raised terraces around the old baseball pitcher's area known as 'Catcher's Corner', latterly replaced by the Osmaston Stand. The football club purchased the stadium on 9 March 1925 for £10,400 and immediately began stadium improvements, which meant rebuilding all four stands over the next decade.

Cecil Potter was appointed as the third manager of Derby County during the close season before the 1922/23 season. He is pictured here with his team (middle, inset), who reached the semi-final of FA Cup, losing to West Ham United. The Rams would have gone on to play Bolton Wanderers in the first final to be staged at Wembley. (W.W. Winter Ltd)

The Derby County squad before an away game at Bury on 3 March 1923. Back row, left to right: J. McIntyre, A. Ritchie, B. Olney, H. Thoms, T. Crilly, S. Plackett. Front row: G. Thornewell, J. Lyons, R. Galloway, J. Moore, L. Murphy. The match ended in a 4-1 defeat with George Thornewell scoring the consolation goal.

George Jobey had already made his name in football before becoming Derby's manager in 1925 – he was the first Woolwich Arsenal player to score at Highbury. He managed Derby to promotion in his first year, the 1925/26 season, and then two runners-up positions in the 1929/30 and 1935/36 First Division campaigns. In 1941 he was found guilty of making illegal payments to players as an inducement to sign for the club and was banned for life by the FA. Although the ban was lifted after the war, he only returned for one further year in management at Mansfield.

George Thornewell was a former Rolls-Royce worker and won four England caps before moving to Blackburn Rovers, where he won an FA Cup winners' medal in 1928 – he crossed the ball for one of the fastest goals in FA Cup history. He made his debut for Derby County against Manchester United on 30 August 1919. In all, he made 295 appearances and played in the 1925/26 promotion season. After retiring from professional football he ran the White Hart public house in Duffield where his medals and caps were displayed.

Harry Bedford was born in Derbyshire but his career took him to Nottingham Forest and Blackpool before joining the Rams in September 1925 for £3,500. He scored 160 goals in 203 games before moving on to Newcastle United in 1930. In 1938 he joined the backroom staff at Derby as a masseur. Here he is pictured at the Baseball Ground in the distinctive shirt worn between 1925–27.

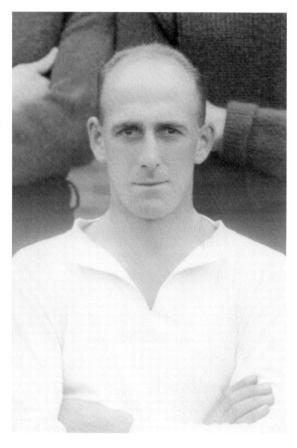

Right: One of Cecil Potter's last signings was Bill Carr, who made 109 appearances in nearly eleven years with the Rams between 1924 and 1935, before joining QPR for £350 in August 1935.

Like many other former players who played for Derby, he had settled in the area; he lived and trained in Derby whilst with QPR. He continued to come and watch his modern counterparts from the Popside.

Opposite bottom: The 1925/26 squad. Back row, left to right: Plackett, Haley, Collins, Rowe, Carr, Olney, Underwood, Bacon. Second row: Bromage (trainer), McIntyre, Wade, McLaverty, Keetley, Davidson, Barratt, Self, Edwards (trainer), Seated: Moore, Wightman, Crilly, Bedford, Thoms, Storer, Fazackerley, Pumford. Front row: Tootle, E. Bromage, Whitehouse, Murphy, Thornewell.

Note that the shirts have a badge for the first time – created by the supporters' club and contained three sections: a rose and crown; buck in the park and a ram's head. This design lasted for two years and a new badge appeared in 1947.

Above, left: George Jobey paid £2,500 to sign Tom Cooper from Port Vale in March 1926. The distinctive white-haired full-back was capped 15 times for England whilst with Derby. He was sold to Liverpool for £7,500 in 1934 after making 267 appearances. Tom met a tragic end as a despatch rider in the military police in June 1940. After this tragic accident, motor-cycle helmets became compulsory for despatch riders.

Above, right: Sammy Crooks signed from Durham City for £300 in 1927 and, on 10 September, was thrown into the first team against Leicester City, following an injury to George Thornewell, after just three reserve team appearances and one colt game.

He was capped on 26 occasions for England before the emergence of Stanley Matthews. Injury meant that he was unfit to play in the 1946 FA Cup final, giving Reg Harrison his opportunity. In all, he made 445 appearances for the Rams, scoring 111 goals.

The Derby County squad for the 1927/28 season. Back row, left to right: W. Bromage, S. Crooks, J. Robson, Boden, C. Rance, A. Bacon, Mann, W. Robson, G. Malloch, F. Jessop, J. Webb, J. Randle, L. Edwards. Middle row: T. Crilly, D. Feraday, R. Barclay, T. Pearson, M. O'Brien, W. Carr, B. Olney, T. Cooper, A. Scott, H. Wilkes, Richie, T. Ruddy. Front row: H. Whiteman, J. McIntyre, G. Thornewell, H. Bedford, J. Gill, H. Thoms, G. Jobey (manager), T. Davison, B. McLaverty, H. Storer, J. Whitehouse, L. Murphy, G. Mee.

Right: George Stephenson, sporting his England shirt and cap, joined Derby from Aston Villa in 1927. He had an excellent goalscoring record of 56 goals in 120 games and was surprisingly sold to Sheffield Wednesday in February 1931.

Below: The Derby County squad for the 1932/33 season. Inset: Tom Cooper, Albert Alderman. Back row, left to right: Syd Wileman, Harry Wilkes, Ralph Hann, Ossie Bowden, Jack Kirby, Jack Nicholas, Jack Robson, Frank Eckersley, Keith Hague. Middle row: Laurie Edwards (trainer), Jack Bowers, Archie Scott, A.H. Fabian, Arnold Robinson, Jack Barker, Eddie Green, George Collin, Bill Bromage (assistant trainer), Front row: Ike Keen, Sid Reid, Norman Robson, Freddie Jessop, George Jobey (manager), Bill Carr, Jimmy Randall, Duncan Hutchison, Dally Duncan. Seated: Jack Webb, Sammy Crooks, Peter Ramage, Eddie Dickendon. (W.W. Winter Ltd)

Jack Bowers leaps above the Manchester City defence during the FA Cup semi-final at Huddersfield, 18 March 1933. Goals by Fabian and Crooks were not enough as the Rams went down 3-2.

Steve Bloomer was employed as a general assistant around the club and he is seen here making a point to Wileman, Crooks, Duncan, Nicholas, Barker and Bowers.

A fishing trawler, number GY154, was built in Middlesbrough and took the name *Derby County*. Her maiden voyage was on 13 September 1933. The Admiralty bought the boat in 1939 and converted it into an anti-submarine vessel. After the war it was re-registered as a fishing boat and eventually scrapped in Belgium during February 1964.

The Derby County squad for the 1934/35 season, back row. Left to right: Ted Roberts, Nicholson, Donald Bird, Dave Bell, Ted Udall, Alan Hughes, Tom Pearson, Webster, Jack Kirby, Vincent Blore, George Hannah, Ralph Hann, Jack Webb, H. Wright, Arnold Robinson, John Philbin. Middle row: Dave Willis (trainer), G. Lowe, Keith Hague, Sid Reid, George Collin, Jack Nicholas, Jack Barker, Jack Bowers, Freddie Jessop, Ossie Bowden, Jock Rafferty, Bill Carr, David Halford, Jimmy Hagan, Bill Bromage (assistant trainer). Front row: T. Lisle, Jimmy Randall, Reg Stockill, Sammy Crooks, Tom Cooper, Peter Ramage, George Jobey (manager), Dally Duncan, Arthur Groves, Arthur Dobbs, Syd Wileman, Ike Keen. (W.W. Winter Ltd)

After making his debut in 1930, Jack Kirby became first-choice goalkeeper in December 1932 and made 191 appearances for the Rams. He is probably best remembered for his refusal to give the Nazi salute during an end of season tour to Germany in May 1934, after the British Foreign Office had advised against causing any political controversy. He is seen here practising at the Baseball Ground, before the Osmaston Stand was built. (Courtesy of Derby Evening Telegraph and www.picturethepast.org.uk

The FA Cup tie at Millwall, 20 February 1937. Derby goalkeeper Scattergood makes an early save with defenders Jack Howe and Ike Keen watching on. The crowd of 48,672 took advantage of any view, however dangerous, some even perching on top of the scoreboard. Millwall won 2-1 against the Rams' team of Scattergood, Bell, Howe, Nicholas, Barker, Keen, Crooks, Stockill, Astley, Napier and Duncan.

Right: Jack Nicholas, the son of former Derby defender William 'Jack' Nicholas, made his debut during the 1928/29 season and made nearly 400 appearances for the Rams. A club stalwart, from September 1931 he missed three games until end of the 1938/39 season. He played in a number of positions, ultimately settling at right-back and had a reputation as a rugged, tough defender. He was responsible for keeping the club going during the Second World War and remains the only man to captain Derby to a FA Cup final victory.

Opposite, below: The 1935/36 squad were runners-up in the L eague Championship, finishing eight points behind Arsenal; Hughie Gallacher (middle of those seated on the floor) was top scorer for the second successive season. The opening of the Normanton Stand completed the redevelopment of the stadium and allowed a new record attendance of 37,380 to attend the FA Cup tie against Nottingham Forest. Derby's reserve team also won the Central League title for the first time.

The Derby County squad for the 1938/39 season. Back row, left to right: M. Sullivan, Ralph. Hann, George. Wilcox, Harry Travis, D. Smart, Tom Alton, Jack Parr, Jack Nicholas. Middle row: Dave Willis (trainer), Leslie. Bailey, David Bell, G. Bramley, Frank Boulton, Harry Wright, H. Wood, Frank King, Jack Barker, Jack. Howe, Bill Bromage (assistant trainer). Front row: Steve McLachlan, Verdun Jones, Alf Jeffries, Jimmy Hagan, Ronnie Dix, Dai Astley, Tommy Eggleston, Chick Musson, T. Bradbury, Tim Ward. Front row: O. Johnson, Jack Brinton, Sammy Crooks, Reg Stockill, T. Lisle, Bertie Mee, H. Jones, Dally Duncan, J. Thompson.

Interestingly, Bertie Mee became famous in the 1970/71 season when he managed Arsenal to a league and FA Cup double. Also, Jimmy Hagan managed the Benfica team when Derby met them in the second round of the European Cup in 1972. (W. W. Winter Ltd)

Upon the onset of the Second World War, league fixtures were suspended after three matches of the 1939/40 season, Derby having won two and lost one of their games. Derby's last pre-war team, selected for a 1-0 win over Aston Villa, was: Boulton, Wilcox, Howe, Nicholas, Barker, Ward, Walsh, Redfern, McCulloch, Stamps and Duncan. (W. W. Winter Ltd)

three

The 1946
FA Cup Final

Derby County played against Birmingham City in the FA Cup semi-final at Hillsborough on 23 March 1946. Raich Carter scored the Rams' goal in the 1-1 draw in front of a 65,000-strong crowd. The match-day squad were, back row, left to right: Reg Harrison, Jack Parr, Vic Woodley, Jim Bullions, Leon Leuty, Jack Stamps. Front row: Chick Musson, Raich Carter, Jack Nicholas, Peter Doherty, Dally Duncan. Four days later, a 4-0 win in front of a record-breaking crowd of 80,407 booked Derby's first Wembley appearance.

Derby spent the week before the FA Cup final at a Harpenden hotel. Here the Rams squad and management relax with the hotel top brass. Back row, left to right: Duncan, Willis, Carter, McCulloch, Bullions, Howe, Nicholas, Stamps, Doherty, Cholerton (director). Front row: Harrison, Woodley, Morrison, Leuty, Crooks, McMillan (manager), the hotel owners, Wassell (director).

Jack Parr, who broke his arm three weeks before the final, being presented to King George VI before the start of the match. He is introduced by captain Jack Nicholas and watched by trainer Willis. Note the 'portable' camera in the foreground.

Raich Carter's shot grazes the crossbar with the Charlton goalkeeper Sam Bartram beaten.

Charlton's goalkeeper Sam Bartram saves a shot from Dally Duncan.

The ball crosses the goal line as a shot from Duncan deflects off Charlton's Bert Turner (seen falling) for the opening goal of the final. Jack Stamps turns away to celebrate. Shortly afterwards, Turner scored at the right end to make the score 1-1.

Peter Doherty darts in front of Duncan to score Derby's second goal.

Peter Doherty goes down in the penalty area and appeals in vain for a penalty kick.

Jack Stamps scores the first of his extra-time goals, splitting the defence of Shreeve and Oakes and comprehensively beating goalkeeper Bartram. Other Derby players in the picture are the rest of the forward line: Carter, Doherty and Duncan.

A match ticket from the 1946 Cup Final, with an original cost of 3s 6d. If you wanted to purchase a ticket stub in good condition, the cost would be between £60–£100 today.

Raich Carter's cup winners medal, purchased by the club from his family before his caps and medals went to auction. This is on display at Pride Park.

Jack Nicholas coming down the steps at Wembley after receiving the FA Cup for the only time in the club's history.

Jack Howe and Leon Leuty help carry captain Jack Nicholas shoulder-high around the Wembley pitch after collecting the cup. Musson is carrying the base of the trophy.

Above: Meanwhile, back in Derby, the council gardeners at Osmaston Park came up with this unique design as a floral tribute to the victory.

Left: This is the programme cover from the game, which originally cost *6d*, and is the prized possession of many Derby fans. Reproductions can be purchased for £15 but genuine copies can generally be purchased at auction with typical prices around £150–£200.

four

The Third Division and Back, 1944–67

The Derby County squad for the 1944/45 season, featuring some 'guest' players that were regularly used during wartime matches. Back row, left to right: Magner (manager), Bullions, Crooks, Leuty, Savage, Nicholas, Trim, Willis (trainer). Front row: Cholerton (director), Robshaw (chairman), Jones, Carter, Lyman, Doherty, Duncan, Walker (director), Catterall (secretary). Kneeling are Parr and Musson.

Crooks, Nicholas and Duncan celebrate after winning the 1944/45 Midland Cup. The Rams had beaten Aston Villa by a 9-0 aggregate scoreline, with Peter Doherty scoring five goals in the second leg. The team for the second leg was Grant, Nicholas, Parr, Bullions, Leuty, Baxter, Crooks, Powell, Jordan, Doherty, Duncan. The second-leg attendance was 16,218 and the match ball from the game is currently displayed at Pride Park.

Derby's forwards for the league game against West Bromwich Albion on 8 December 1945 at the Baseball Ground were Reg Harrison, Raich Carter, Dave McCulloch, Peter Doherty and Dally Duncan. The first three scored the goals in a 3-3 draw in front of 29,018. Bomb damage from the Second World War can still be seen on the top tier of the Osmaston Stand.

Derby players arriving at the airport in Prague during May 1946 for an end of season tour. The Rams played four matches in eleven days against AC Sparta (lost 3-2), Zidenice Brno (won 2-0), Bratislava (lost 3-1) and Slavia Prague (lost 3-1).

Above left: Jack Stamps scored twice on his debut in March 1938 after signing from New Brighton. He was a no-nonsense centre forward who later suffered blindness but still attended every home game whenever possible. Stamps scored two goals in the 1946 Cup final and was always greeted warmly when he attended club events. He had a testimonial game at Derby in 1969.

Above right: Raich Carter pictured in action during October 1946. Carter was signed by Derby from Sunderland while stationed with the RAF at Loughborough during the war. It was here that the Carter-Doherty partnership began; Derby ultimately had two of the finest forwards of the era. Carter stayed with Derby until 1948 when he moved to become player-manager at Hull City.

The Derby County squad for the 1946/47 season. Back row, left to right: Bullions, Mozley, Grant, Howe, Musson. Front row: Harrison, Ward, Leuty, Morrison, Stamps, K. Powell. Inset: Broome, Carter. This line-up lost 2-0 away to Aston Villa on 4 January 1947.

Above: Derby's forwards – Reg Harrison, Raich Carter, Ron Peart, Jack Stamps and Frank Broome – for the away league match at Blackpool on 1 February 1947. Although Carter scored, the team lost 2-1. The complete team was Woodley, Mozley, Howe, Ward, Leuty, Musson, Harrison, Carter, Peart, Stamps, Broome. This was Ron Peart's only appearance for Derby.

Right: Derby broke the British transfer record to sign Billy Steel for £15,500 from Morton in June 1947. Although he was a very skilful player, he was allegedly an awkward teammate; many saw a decline in the team whilst he was with Derby. He was sold to Dundee after three years for a Scottish record fee of £23,000.

Above: Reg Harrison was born in Derby and was fortunate to find himself playing alongside many famous players, such as Carter, Crooks and Doherty, who helped to guide his early career. An injury to Crooks gave him the opportunity to play in the semi-final and final of the 1946 FA Cup. He made 281 appearances and scored 59 goals in his nine-year Rams career. He later returned to the Baseball Ground in the Boston United team that famously won 6-1 in the FA Cup tie 1955 – one of the biggest cup shocks ever.

Left: Jim Bullions joined the Rams from Chesterfield in 1944 and was Derby's youngest player in the 1946 cup final at the age of twenty-two. He only played twenty-nine games for Derby – twelve in the FA Cup – before leaving for Leeds United in November 1947. He is credited, along with Sammy Crooks, with establishing Shrewsbury Town as a league club.

Reg Harrison scores the only goal of the game against Arsenal at the Baseball Ground on 29 November 1947, inflicting Arsenal's first defeat of the season. Derby's team was: Townsend, Mozley, Howe, Ward, Leuty, Musson, Harrison, Carter, Bullions, Steel and McCormick.

Looking from the Osmaston End, the Baseball Ground pictured in 1947 with the main ABC Stand on the right-hand side. The stand sports an advert on the roof for the locally brewed Offilers' Ales.

The heavy Baseball Ground pitch is in evidence during this game against Chelsea in early January 1948, where Reg Harrison shoots in a 5-1 victory.

The ball is in the net on a typically muddy Derby pitch in the 1940s. Raich Carter is on the left, unmarked in the penalty area, and the goalkeeper can only watch as the ball nestles in the corner of the net.

Prior to the 1948 FA Cup semi-final, Derby players appear in a relaxed state of mind. Some of the players pictured are Jack Poole (trainer), Jack Stamps, Chick Musson, Bert Mozley, Raich Carter, Angus Morrison, Jack Howe, Billy Steel, Reg Harrison, Leon Leuty and Tim Ward.

The Derby team that lost the 1948 cup semi-final 3-1 to Manchester United. Back row, left to right: Stuart McMillan (manager), Tim Ward, Bert Mozley, Leon Leuty, Jock Wallace, Jack Howe, Chick Musson, Jack Poole (trainer). Front row: Reg Harrison, Raich Carter, Jack Stamps, Billy Steel, Angus Morrison.

The Derby County squad for the 1948/49 season., Back row, left to right: Bert Mozley, Tim Ward, Leon Leuty, William Townsend, Jack Parr, Chick Musson, John Poppitt. Front row: Reg Harrison, Tommy Powell, Jack Stamps, Jack Howe, Cyril Thompson, Billy Steel, Frank Broome. This was to be Derby's best season until the 1970s. The Rams, who finished third in the First Division, set the British transfer record by signing Johnny Morris from Manchester United for £24,500 and set a record attendance of 51,385 at Portsmouth.

Tommy Powell made his debut in a wartime friendly and broke into the team during the 1948/49 season. He played regularly until 1961, when injury finally forced his retirement after 406 appearances. A one-club player, he was the father of Steve Powell, who played for Derby from 1971 until 1984.

The Derby County squad for the 1950/51 season. Back row, left to right: Poole (trainer), Cushlow, Mozley, Brown, Townsend, Oliver, Parr, Musson, Mays, Bowers (assistant trainer). Middle row: Bell, McLaren, Stamps, McMillan (manager), Lee, Morris, Powell, Parry, Mynard. Front row: Ward, Parkin, Harrison, Walker, McLachlan, Wilkins.

This team lost 5-2 in an away match against Blackburn Rovers on 13 September 1954, during a season that saw them finish bottom of the Second Division. Back row, left to right: Parry, Mozley, Hunter, Upton, Bell, Davies. Front row: Savin, Powell, Barrowcliffe, Dunn, McQuillan.

Ray Straw jointly holds the record with Jack Bowers for the number of league goals scored in one season (37). They came during the promotion season of 1956/57 from the Third Division (North). He made his debut in 1951 in the First Division of the Football League, eventually playing in all six divisions after moving on to Coventry City and Mansfield Town.

Tim Ward was signed from non-league Cheltenham in 1937 and on switching positions from left- to right-wing produced the form that earned him two England caps. After fourteen years on the playing staff he was sold to Barnsley. He became another former player to return as manager in 1962 and was responsible for signing Alan Durban and Kevin Hector.

Irishman Reg Ryan was Harry Storer's first signing in 1955 for £3,000 from West Bromwich Albion as Derby faced life in the Third Division for the first time. He won one cap for the Republic of Ireland and was a major force in getting Derby back into Division Two within two years after 139 appearances and 31 goals.

The Third Division (North) champions for the 1956/57 season. Back row, left to right: J.Bowers (assistant trainer), Martin, Buchanan, Jackson, Brown, Webster, Davies, Clark, R. Hann (trainer). Middle row: Smith, McDonnell, Mays, Oliver, Young, Upton, Fallon, Straw, Crowshaw. The directors are seated. Front row: Darroch, Powell, Parry, Ryan, Darwin, Woodhead.

The Derby County squad for the 1958/59 season. Back row, left to right: Hannigan, Mays, Daykin, Hann (trainer), Brown, Davies, Darwin. Middle row: Hunt, Smith, Barrowcliffe, Oxford, Upton, Adlington, Martin, Powell, Young. Seated: Annable (secretary), Longson, Bates, Paul, Jackson (chairman), King, Walters, Storer (manager). Front row: Woodhead, Ryan, Womack, Parry, Clark, Bowers.

This steam locomotive was built in 1936 and named *Derby County*. It ran passenger services down the East Coast into London until August 1959 when it was scrapped. A replica nameplate is located in Starbucks at Pride Park.

Above: The Derby County squad for the 1959/60 season. Back row, left to right: Barrowcliffe, Mays, Young, Oxford, Smith, Conwell, Upton. Middle row: Storer (manager), Daykin, Parry, Hannigan, Darwin, Thompson, Hann (trainer). Front row: Powell, Davies, Cargill, Brown.

Right: Jack Parry came from a footballing family and joined Derby in 1948. He scored many goals in the 1955/56 season before injury forced him miss a large number of games. He returned as captain in the Second Division, was a regular starter until the mid-1960s and, in all, made 517 appearances; only Kevin Hector appeared in more league matches for the club.

A very early Brian Clough squad from 1967. Back row, left to right: Pat Wright, John Richardson, Peter Daniel, Reg Matthews, Bobby Saxton, Ron Webster, Colin Boulton, Roy McFarland, Phil Waller, Mick Hopkinson. Front row: Gordon Hughes, Alan Durban, Kevin Hector, John O'Hare, Richie Barker, Alan Hinton.

A cheerleader in front of the Osmaston End during the 1960s. From the picture, the crowd is still a predominately male audience. The small metal fencing went around three sides of the pitch, before being replaced by more substantial railings in the 1970s.

five

Trophies
Galore,
1969–76

The Clough and Taylor team at the start of the 1968/69 season. It was not until Willie Carlin joined the squad after four games that results improved and the Rams only lost twice with him in the team. Back row, left to right: Arthur Stewart, John Robson, Les Green, Roy McFarland, Ron Webster, Dave Mackay. Front row: John O'Hare, Kevin Hector, Richie Barker, Jim Walker, Alan Hinton.

A long queue of fans wait patiently in the rain to get their tickets for the League Cup replay against Chelsea in October 1968. Inspired by Mackay's leadership, the Rams won 3-1 and the crowd began to believe that the team was capable of great things.

John O'Hare scores the third goal against Bolton Wanderers from a Hector pass in a 5-1 win on 5 April 1969. The thumping victory secured promotion to the First Division in front of 30,684 delirious supporters. This result was part of a run of nine successive wins and the team on the day was: Green, Webster, Robson, Durban, McFarland, Mackay, Wignall, Carlin, Hector, O'Hare and Hinton.

Les Green is watched by defenders Dave Mackay, Roy McFarland and John Robson in 1969. The old Popside terracing can be seen in the background before the Ley Stand was built over the top of it in the summer of 1969.

Left: Alan Durban was signed from Cardiff City in the summer of 1963. Initially a prolific goalscorer, he evolved into a more orthodox midfield player. He represented Wales on twenty-seven occasions and, in all, he scored goals in 403 appearances in over a decade with the Rams. He returned as assistant-manager to Roy McFarland in 1993.

Below: A guard of honour is made by the Millwall players as Dave Mackay leads out the Second Division champions. A kit mix-up meant that Derby had to play in Millwall's red away shirts. A Willie Carlin goal gave the visitors a 1-0 win.

Before the last match of the season against Bristol City on 19 April 1969, the team were presented with the Second Division trophy and duly paraded it around the pitch for the fans. Derby won the Championship by seven points from Crystal Palace and a substantial thirteen points ahead of third-placed Charlton Athletic; overall they lost only five league matches.

The Rams players and staff show off the Championship trophy on an open-top bus tour of Derby. Taking in the adulation of the crowd are, from left to right: Webster, Robson, McFarland, Hinton, O'Hare, Wignall, Durban, Green and Mackay, who holds the Second Division Championship trophy aloft.

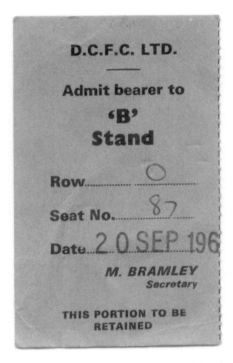

Above, left: Ticket stub from the 'B' Stand for the match against Tottenham Hotspur on 20 September 1969.

Above, right: The match programme from the game against Spurs on 20 September 1969. The match saw Derby's record home attendance of 41,826 cram into the Baseball Ground. This was one of six games during the 1969/70 season that attracted crowds of over 40,000.

Dave Mackay, a former Spurs player, enjoying the game. The final score was 5-0 to Derby with two goals from Alan Durban and one each from Willie Carlin, John O'Hare and Kevin Hector.

Above: Ian Storey-Moore beats Les Green to a cross in the game against Nottingham Forest on 29 November 1969 that the visitors won 2-0. Storey-Moore was paraded in front of the Derby fans thinking they had signed him in March 1972; he had actually signed for Manchester United after Forest refused to sanction the deal. Two months later, Derby were champions.

Right: Kevin Hector was signed from Bradford Park Avenue by Tim Ward for a fee of £40,000 in 1966 – it was a lot of money for an average Second Division club at the time. He nearly became a national hero when a last-minute shot was cleared off the Polish line in a World Cup qualifying game in 1974, one of his two substitute appearances for England – he is one of Derby's greatest players.

Setting off on a pre-season training run at Nottingham Racecourse before the start of the 1970/71 season. The squad is led by Gordon Guthrie and Jeff Bourne. Also in the leading group is Dave Mackay with Boulton, Durban, Webster, Hector and Hinton at the rear. (Courtesy of the *Derby Evening Telegraph* and www.picturethepast.org.uk)

Dave Mackay holds the Watney Cup aloft having just beaten Manchester United 4-1 in the inaugural final of this short-lived competition. Derby had beaten Fulham and Sheffield United to reach the final. The trophy is still retained by the club.

Above: The Baseball Ground directors' box during a league game. Along the front row are, from right to left: Peter Taylor, Alan Hinton, Brian Clough, Sam Longson, Sir Robertson King, Sidney Bradley, Rudd, Frank Innes, Sir Alf Ramsey (the incumbent England manager) and Michael Keeling.

Right: Colin Todd joined the Rams for a British-record £170,000 transfer fee from Sunderland in February 1971. He was seen as the long-term replacement for Dave Mackay. The classy defender was PFA Player of the Year in 1974/75 and made 27 appearances for England. He had a brief spell as manager of the club in 2002. His son, Andy (born in Derby), also signed for Derby at the start of the 2007/08 season.

Dave Mackay is presented with the Player of the Year trophy before his last match as a Derby player against West Bromwich Albion on 1 May 1971. Mackay left to become player-manager at Swindon Town. Looking on is the player who would take his place in the team, Colin Todd.

Alan Durban's ability to arrive late and unmarked in the penalty area often resulted in a goal. Here he scores the second goal in the 3-1 defeat of Manchester City on 4 December 1971. This win took Derby up to second place in the First Division.

Right: In 1970 Terry Hennessey followed Hinton and Wignall from Nottingham Forest to become Derby's first £100,000 transfer. An experienced Welsh international, he suffered several injuries that restricted him to 82 appearances in three years.

Below: Brian Clough and Peter Taylor signed new contracts for the Rams in 1969. Chairman Sydney Bradley sits between them as the rest of the Derby board look on. (Courtesy of *Derby Evening Telegraph* and www.picturethepast.org.uk)

Left: Alan Durban receiving the Texaco Cup from Len Shipman, Chairman of the Football League. Derby had beaten Dundee United, Stoke and Newcastle before playing Airdrie in a two-legged final. Goals from Davies and a Hinton penalty gave Derby a 2-1 victory.

Below: A lucky escape this time as a John O'Hare effort rebounds off the bar: Crystal Palace were outclassed and easily defeated 3-0 on 6 November 1971, with McFarland and Gemmill watching from the stands.

The last match of the season, on 1 May 1972, against Liverpool, was a tight game with this McGovern goal, scored on the hour from the edge of the area, the difference between the teams. (Courtesy of *Derby Evening Telegraph* and www.picturethepast.org.uk)

The directors celebrate winning the 1971/72 Championship with a glass of champagne on Tuesday 9 May. The Championship victory was sealed after the previous evening's results, with Leeds losing at Wolves and Liverpool drawing at Arsenal. Assistant-Secretary John Howarth pours a glass of bubbly for Rudd, Bradley, King and Longson.

After the Liverpool game the players had gone to Cala Millor to get away from things. Jim Walker, Colin Boulton, Ron Webster, Alan Hinton and John Robson enjoy themselves. (Courtesy of *Derby Evening Telegraph* and www.picturethepast.org.uk)

Outside the Baseball Ground, preparations are underway for the arrival of the players to receive the trophy, Sunday 14 May 1972. (Copyright Garth Jones)

The players are led out by Alan Hinton and John McGovern to meet the awaiting Derby County fans who are in celebratory mood. (Copyright Garth Jones)

Jim Walker, John O'Hare, Ron Webster, Colin Boulton, Kevin Hector, Archie Gemmill (all standing) with John Robson and John McGovern (back to camera) show off the Texaco Cup and Championship trophy to a group of supporters. (Copyright Garth Jones)

Two major players of the Championship-winning team were missing from the celebrations, as Roy McFarland and Colin Todd were both on duty with England. Pictured with trophies are, back row, left to right: Sheridan (coach), Hinton, Hennessey, Gemmill, Daniel, Guthrie, Taylor, Longson, Walker, Boulton, Gordon (trainer). Front row: McGovern, O'Hare, Durban, Hector, Robson, Webster. The trophies are the Football League Championship, the Central League Championship and the Texaco Cup. (Copyright Garth Jones)

Brian Clough takes the Championship trophy over to the packed Popside and Ley Stand. (Copyright Garth Jones)

Above: It was a heroes'
welcome for the Derby
players as 16,000 fans
turned out early on the
Sunday morning to see
the official presentation of
the Championship trophy,
as well as the Texaco Cup
and Central League titles.
(Copyright Garth Jones)

Right: Crowds surround
the Council House and
block the roads as the
players and management
make their way to a civic
reception. (Courtesy of *Derby
Evening Telegraph* and www.
picturethepast.org.uk)

Brian Clough appears on the balcony with the Championship trophy.

Above left: An official 1971/72 autograph sheet produced at the start of the season. Few would have believed that in just nine months' time these same players would become household names, take the First Division title and enter into the European Cup.

Above right: August 1972 saw the Rams heading into European competitions for the first time. UEFA regulations and the demands of colour television meant that the floodlights at the Baseball Ground that had been installed the in the 1950s on some crude scaffolding were inadequate. They were replaced by state-of-the-art pylons and lights. These lights were still in use when the Baseball Ground was last used for first-team matches in 1997. (Courtesy of *Derby Evening Telegraph* and www.picturethepast.org.uk)

Being League champions meant that European club competition would grace the Baseball Ground for the first time. Back row, left to right: Clough, Hennessey, Webster, Boulton, Todd, Robson, Taylor, Gordon (trainer). Front row: McGovern, Gemmill, O'Hare, McFarland, Hector, Hinton, Durban.

David Nish makes his Derby debut on 26 August 1972 and is tackled in an unorthodox manner by a Norwich forward in a 1-0 defeat. Looking on are Jim Walker and Alan Durban.

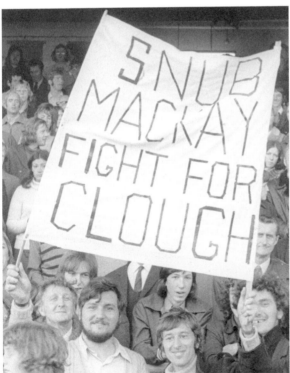

Above: Derby and Leeds both played in their change kits for the FA Cup sixth-round tie at the Baseball Ground on 17 March 1973. Derby wore all blue and Leeds all red. Kevin Hector is seen taking on Paul Madeley but a Nish own-goal gave Leeds the win on their way to the final.

Left: After a long running battle with Chairman Sam Longson, the unthinkable happened when Clough and Taylor resigned in October 1973. The influential pair were replaced by Dave Mackay and his assistant Des Anderson. A supporters' movement was started to get the management pair to return and there was almost a players' strike. (Courtesy of *Derby Evening Telegraph* and www.picturethepast.org.uk)

John McGovern (centre) and Kevin Hector watch McGovern's long-range header beat Leicester City's Peter Shilton for the winning goal on 20 October 1973. In the first match after Clough's departure, Hector scored Derby's other goal in a 2-1 win as part of the team picked by Jimmy Gordon. (Courtesy of *Derby Evening Telegraph* and www.picturethepast.org.uk)

A team picture taken soon after Mackay had taken over in October 1973. Back row, left to right: Gordon, Todd, O'Hare, Powell, Daniel, Boulton, Webster, Davies, Thomas, Anderson. Front row: Nish, McGovern, Gemmill, Mackay, McFarland, Hector, Hinton, Newton.

The Derby County squad for the 1974/75 season; the Rams finished as champions of England.
Back row, left to right: Guthrie, Thomas, Daniel, Webster, Moseley, Boulton, Hinton, Todd, Nish,
Hector, Anderson. Front row: Davies, Bourne, Gemmill, McFarland, Webb, Longson, Mackay, Lee,
Powell, Newton, Rioch.

John O'Hare, playing for Leeds after his transfer from Derby, is watched by Peter Daniel. A late
goal from Francis Lee gave won the game played on 2 December 1974. The Rams were not to
win at Leeds again until Novemner 2007.

Hector scores one of his three goals against QPR in a comfortable 5-2 win on 9 November 1974. The other goals came from Lee and Rioch. It was an excellent result as the Rams had played a midweek UEFA Cup match in Madrid that went to extra-time and penalties.

The Rams inflicted a 5-0 defeat on the Hatters over the 1975 Easter period, as Roger Davies scored all five goals in the game. Steve Buckley, the Luton left-back, fails to stop the out-of-picture Davies' second strike.

An Alan Hinton corner on 66 minutes reaches Bruce Rioch, whose shot goes into the West Ham net on 12 April 1975 during the penultimate home game of the 1974/75 season. This win took Derby to the top of the table for the first time.

Before the last league game of the season against Carlisle United, the players were presented with Championship trophy. A lacklustre 0-0 draw was played out in front of 36,882 spectators on 26 April 1975. Nish and Hector celebrate in front on the Normanton Stand with the Championship trophy.

Above: Peter Daniel joined Derby in 1963 but his opportunities were limited to the odd appearance filling in for injuries. His big break came as a result of a serious injury to Roy McFarland, sustained whilst playing for England. During the 1974/75 season he filled McFarland's shoes admirably and was voted the Player of the Year.

Right: Kevin Hector was a prolific scorer for the Rams, scoring against European giants Benfica and Juventus, as well as one in the 1975 Charity Shield. He holds the all-time appearance record of 589 for Derby, which is unlikely to be beaten and is second behind Bloomer in the all-time goalscoring list, with 201.

The Championship-winning squad on the pitch before the match against Carlisle United. Back row, left to right: Anderson, Mackay, Davies, Newton, Longson, Boulton, McFarland, Hinton, Lee, Webster, Nish, Daniel, Todd, Powell, Guthrie. Front row: Thomas, Rioch, Gemmill, Hector.

At the end of the 1974/75 season, the pitch was replaced and pieces of the turf were packaged and sold in commemorative pouches. This publicity picture shows Chairman Sam Longson digging up the penalty spot at the Osmaston End of the stadium.

A staff party at the Palm Court Restaurant, Allestree, 1975. At the head of the table is Sam Longson, with Mackay, Anderson and Webb on the right.

After missing the majority of the Championship season, Roy McFarland made a dramatic return to the scene of his injury at Wembley by scoring Derby's second goal in the Charity Shield win against West Ham United on 9 August 1975.

59,000 fans, mainly from the Midlands, had seen Derby lift the Charity Shield in new signing Charlie George's first appearance. Pictured parading the shield are George, Thomas, Newton, McFarland, Gemmill, Rioch, Nish and Hector.

The squad proudly showing off the Championship trophy at the Baseball Ground in the special shirts that were worn for the Charity Shield. Back row, left to right: Anderson, Webster, Daniel, Todd, Boulton, Moseley, Bourne, Powell, Thomas, Newton, Hector, Guthrie. Front row: Lee, George, Rioch, McFarland, Mackay, Gemmill, Nish, Davies, Hinton.

Above: Derby substitute Davies is fouled by Thompson on the edge of the area but no penalty is given – not an unusual event for the away team at Anfield. Shortly afterwards, another penalty appeal was turned down as the score finished 1-1 on 29 October 1975.

Right: Colin Boulton had been at Derby since 1964 but it was not until late 1970 that he was given an extended run in the side. That run, however, included every league game of both First Division-winning campaigns. His 344 appearances are the most by any goalkeeper in the club's history. He was sold during Tommy Docherty's reign and his career was cut short with a broken leg whilst with Lincoln City. (Courtesy of *Derby Evening Telegraph* and www.picturethepast.org.uk)

Charlie George scores a penalty against Liverpool on 28 February 1976, with Henry Newton and Liverpool's Ian Callaghan in the background. One point separated the top four teams – Liverpool, QPR, Manchester United and Derby.

Looking along Shaftesbury Street from the Baseball Hotel, the terraced houses can be seen prior to being demolished. These houses made way for the official club car park soon afterwards.

Right: Rod Thomas had already won a League Cup winners' medal with Swindon Town and was Mackay's first signing. He had to wait for an injury to the reliable Ron Webster before he got a first-team opportunity. He won 19 caps for Wales whilst with Derby.

Below: Just three days after losing at Real Madrid, the Rams played away at Arsenal on 8 November 1975. After 25 minutes, a goal by Hector, set up by George and Lee, gave Derby a 1-0 win. Note the popular 'Argentina'-style away kit.

David Nish tussles with former Derby trainee Phil Boyer, who was a prolific goalscorer with Bournemouth and Norwich. Derby paid a British record fee of £250,000 to sign Nish from Leicester City in August 1972.

Charlie George was captured from Arsenal during the summer of 1975 as he was about to sign for Tottenham and made his competitive debut in the Charity Shield game at Wembley. A favourite with the fans, he made a brief return in 1982 to fight relegation. A dislocated shoulder days before the FA Cup semi-final in 1976 perhaps marked the start of the club's decline in the late 1970s. (Courtesy of *Derby Evening Telegraph* and www.picturethepast.org.uk)

six

European
Adventures

The home fans hold up a banner in English during Derby's European Cup quarter-final against Spartak Trnava in modern-day Slovakia. Although the Slovaks won the first leg 1-0, on 7 March 1973, Derby overpowered them 2-0 in the second leg at the Baseball Ground.

Kevin Hector, scorer of both goals in the second leg, is tackled by a Spartak defender.

Above: Part of the crowd at the Stadio Comunale stadium in Turin that greeted the Derby and Juventus players in the semi-final first leg. Rumours that the match officials were bribed by the 'Old Lady' infuriated the Derby hierarchy.

Right: This rare VIP-edition programme is for the return leg of the semi-final. An Alan Hinton missed penalty and Roger Davies' dismissal sealed Derby's exit from the competition. The Juventus team included the current England manager, Fabio Capello.

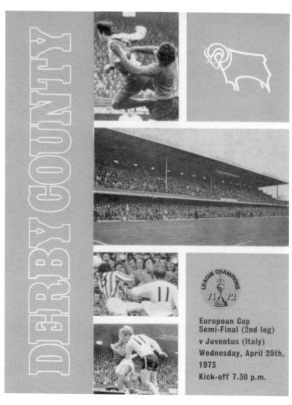

DERBY COUNTY

European Cup
Semi-Final (2nd leg)
v Juventus (Italy)
Wednesday, April 25th,
1973
Kick-off 7.30 p.m.

The captains shake hands and exchange pennants before the home leg of the European Cup match with Real Madrid on 22 October 1975.

The opening goal, after just 10 minutes, saw a low cross from Archie Gemmill met on the volley by Charlie George. Francis Lee, on the right of the picture, turns in delight. Possibly one of the most famous goals at the Baseball Ground.

Charlie George completes his hat-trick with this penalty that sent goalkeeper Miguel Angel the wrong way. Derby's other goal came from Nish in the 4-1 victory.

Specialist first-day covers were produced for some of Derby's matches; this rare example was flown back from Madrid. These covers were produced in the UK by Dawn Covers of Stockport and those that were stamped and franked in Spain are particularly rare.

Over 126,000 people were present at the Santiago Bernebeu to witness the Rams collapse to a 5-1 extra-time defeat to Real Madrid on Bonfire Night 1975. It is still the largest crowd that have seen a Derby County match. The Derby fans who were there saw Roger Davies just miss a superb cross by Alan Hinton with mere minutes of normal time to go.

Above: Derby recorded their biggest ever win, a 12–0 score against Irish side Finn Harps, on 15 September 1976. Hector converts the tenth goal; he scored five in all, with hat-tricks for George and James, and one from Rioch.

Left: This is probably the most sought-after Derby County programme of the last sixty years from the UEFA Cup tie against AEK Athens in 1976. The flimsy four-page programme has rarely emerged for sale on the open market.

seven

Back to the Top, 1976–96

Derby were without a league win when they met Spurs in mid-October 1977. Four goals from Bruce Rioch, and further strikes from George (2), Todd and Thomas, completed an astonishing 8-2 win. Rioch lies flat out after scoring the fifth goal, a diving header.

Gerry Daly tries to deliver a cross against Nottingham Forest at the Baseball Ground but his effort is blocked by ex-Ram Archie Gemmill. Derby's team, in a 0-0 draw on 14 January 1978, was Middleton, Langan, Buckley, Rioch, Daniel, Todd, Curran, Daly, Masson, George and Ryan (sub. Powell).

Steve Buckley's first goal for the Rams came against the already-relegated Leicester City on 22 April 1978 in a 4-1 win. This came after ex-Ram Roger Davies had given Leicester the lead on 57 minutes.

The Derby squad for the 1979/80 season. Back row, left to right: Colin Addison (manager), Dave Swindlehurst, Steve Powell, Keith Osgood, Jakka Banovic, Steve Cherry, Roger Jones, Alan Ramage, Roy McFarland, Jonathan Clark, John Newman (assistant-manager), Gordon Guthrie (physio). Front row: Glenn Skivington, Alan Biley, Paul Emson, Barry Powell, Kevin Wilson, Steve Buckley, Steve Emery.

Gerry Daly scoring after a Peter Shilton fumble in the victory over their fiercest rivals, Nottingham Forest. Forest were reigning European Champions when they visited the Baseball Ground on 24 November 1979. The form book was dramatically torn up as Derby, who were relegated at the end of the season, trounced their local rivals 4-1.

Alan Biley chips the ball into the net to give Derby a 3-1 lead against Sheffield Wednesday on 4 October 1980. The long-haired Biley was sold to Everton later that season. The team for this match was Jones, Emery, Buckley, S. Powell, McFarland, Osgood, Clark, B. Powell, Biley, Swindlehurst and Emson.

Kevin Hector rises above the Luton Town defence to head home in a 2-2 draw. Hector re-signed for the Rams in October 1980 to be part of a rebuilt side put together by Colin Addison following the previous season's relegation.

Derby County and Nottingham Forest were paired in the third round of the FA Cup and the match was billed as 'Clough *v.* Taylor'. An Archie Gemmill free-kick put Derby into the lead before Andy Hill – ironically a Forest fan – clipped the ball over goalkeeper Sutton late in the game to complete a famous victory on 8 January 1983.

John Barton scores his only goal for Derby with this effort in the closing minutes of a 1-1 draw at Leicester City on 5 March 1983. Derby were in relegation trouble for most of the season – only an unbeaten run of 15 games in 1983 under manager Peter Taylor secured Second Division football for another year.

At the start of the centenary year in 1984 many famous players from previous eras attended various celebratory functions. Amongst the attendees were George Thornewell (1919–1927), Jack Stamps (1938–1953) and Raich Carter (1945–1947). (Courtesy of *Derby Evening Telegraph* and www.picturethepast.org.uk)

The launch of the centenary celebrations in November 1983. Back row, left to right: McFarland, Davison, Wilson, Powell, Daniel, Barrowcliffe, Upton, Oxford, Straw, Powell, Young, Morrison, Guthrie. Front row: Thornewell, Webb, Jeffries, Carter, Stamps, Ward, Ryan, Harrison, Carlin.

Action from the FA Cup fourth-round tie against Telford United on 1 February 1984. Bobby Davison chips the ball over the goalkeeper to complete his hat trick in a 3-2 win. The team for this match was Cherry, Barton, Buckley, Gemmill, Watson, Powell, Futcher, Davison, Wilson, Plummer and Robertson.

Derby fans at Plymouth for the FA Cup quarter-final in March 1984. Derby were in financial trouble and just days away from receiving a winding-up order in the High Court. The cup provided the only highlight in a poor year that led to relegation to the Third Division. The result was 0-0 but they lost at home in the replay and missed out on a semi-final against Watford. (Courtesy of *Derby Evening Telegraph* and www. picturethepast.org.uk)

Archie Gemmill made over 400 appearances for Derby in two spells, his last home game coming against Portsmouth on 9 May 1984. Peter Taylor had brought him back to Derby as one of his first signings. (Courtesy of *Derby Evening Telegraph* and www. picturethepast.org.uk)

The 1984/85 season was Derby's centenary year and they found themselves in the Third Division for the first time since the mid-1950s. As well as a special centenary kit sponsored by Bass, the brewer also brought out a special centenary ale. (Courtesy of *Derby Evening Telegraph* and www.picturethepast.org.uk)

Kenny Burns heads in a John Robertson corner for the second goal in a 2-0 win over Lincoln City in the Third Division on 29 September 1984. The team that day was: John Burridge, Charlie Palmer, Steve Buckley, Steve Powell, Floyd Streete, Kenny Burns, Kevin Taylor, Kevin Wilson, Bobby Davison, Paul Hooks and John Robertson (sub. Paul Richardson).

Local boy Steve Buckley arrived at Derby in 1978 from Luton Town and was probably the one success of the Tommy Docherty reign. A tough tackling left-back, he had a tremendous shot and was a regular penalty-taker, cracking this one in against Ipswich Town in the Milk Cup during October 1984.

Steve Powell, now in his thirteenth season with Derby, scores with a powerful header in an away match at Cambridge United on 1 December 1984. Powell is seen wearing the special centenary shirt. Also in the picture are Bobby Davison (extreme left) and Kevin Taylor (centre).

Gary Micklewhite's lob crosses the line to give Derby the lead in a 3-1 win away at York City in the Third Division encounter on 8 February 1986. The ball is watched by fellow Derby forwards Trevor Christie (extreme left) and Jeff Chandler.

Two points were needed from the last two matches of the season to seal promotion. Trevor Christie scores a late penalty kick to give a 2-1 win against Rotherham United on 9 May 1986 and send Derby up. Substitute Phil Gee had scored the opening goal on 77 minutes. It was quickly cancelled out but Christie removed any doubts with the spot kick.

Above left: Michael Dunford originally joined the administration staff in 1969 and left some twenty-five years later in November 1994. He had performed many jobs behind the scenes from assistant secretary to general manager and, ultimately, chief executive. He later moved to Everton and is currently chief executive at Plymouth Argyle. He is pictured here with new director Mick McGarry before the season's opening game against Oldham on 23 August 1986.

Above right: Bobby Davison came to Derby's attention when playing for Halifax Town against them in the League Cup in 1982. Peter Taylor, the manager at the time, signed him and he became a prolific scorer in the lower leagues but was unable to repeat that success at the highest level. He returned on loan from Leeds in 1991 and, with over 100 Rams goals to his name, was a huge fans' favourite.

Mark Wallington in front of the travelling fans during a 1-1 draw at Plymouth in December 1986. He was first-choice goalkeeper during successive promotions, until replaced by Peter Shilton.

A 2-0 victory over Leeds United sealed a second successive promotion for the Rams on 2 May 1987. The squad wa, back row, left to right: Guthrie, Lillis, Gregory, Williams, Forsyth, MacLaren, Pratley, Blades, Cross, Sage, McFarland. Front row: Steele, Gee, Cox, Hindmarch, Davison, Callaghan, Micklewhite, Harbey.

Derby needed to win their last match of the 1986/87 season, at home against Plymouth Argyle, to secure the Championship trophy. Having gone behind to the visitors, they eventually overcame them 4-2. Nigel Callaghan scored the second goal after a long solo run following a Plymouth corner. (Courtesy of *Derby Evening Telegraph* and www.picturethepast.org.uk)

The Derby County first team after the game with Plymouth confirmed the Rams as Second Division champions for the 1986/87 season. Back row, left to right: John Gregory, Roy McFarland (assistant-manager), Gordon Guthrie (trainer), Bobby Davison, Ross MacLaren, Paul Blades, Mark Lillis, Michael Forsyth. Front row: Phil Gee, Gary Micklewhite, Rob Hindmarch, Arthur Cox (manager), Nigel Callaghan, Eric Steele, Geraint Williams.

Left: Geraint 'George' Williams collecting the Player of the Year trophy from manager Arthur Cox in 1987. Williams was signed from Bristol Rovers and proved an exceptionally useful defensive-midfield player who went on to win many caps for Wales in his time at Derby and Ipswich. As a manager he led Colchester to the second tier of English football for the first time in their history.

Below: The Derby County squad, back in the First Division, at the start of the 1987/88 season. Back row, left to right: McFarland, MacLaren, Forsyth, Gregory, Taylor, Pratley, Shilton, Hindmarch, Wallington, Garner, Lillis, Blades, Guthrie. Front row: McCord, Callaghen, Williams, Sage, Cross, Gee, Cox, Davison, Micklewhite, Lewis, Penney, Briscoe, McClaren.

Right: Steve McClaren was bought by Arthur Cox in 1985 from Hull City. Injuries did not help his Derby career, as he was unable to force his way past John Gregory and after thirty-odd appearances was sold to Bristol City. He returned to Derby as first-team coach under Jim Smith and was immediately successful. McClaren left to join Manchester United as assistant-manager to Sir Alex Ferguson and was integral to their 1999 treble season success. Later he became a manager in his own right at Middlesbrough and assistant to Sven Goran Eriksson with the national team, which led to an unsuccessful period as coach of England.

Below: Owner Robert Maxwell seen in discussion with manager Arthur Cox and Managing Director Stuart Webb in the Baseball Ground changing room on 26 September 1987. This was Maxwell's first visit to the stadium for a league match against another Maxwell family-owned club, Oxford United, and also coincided with the clubs 101st AGM.

Above: Arthur Cox welcomes the Nottingham Forest manager, Brian Clough, to the Baseball Ground in October 1987. During Cox's nine-year reign at Derby, the two clubs played each other nine times in league matches, winning just once in November 1990.

Left: John Gregory joined Derby when they were in the Third Division; his experience and skill led to successive promotions. He was joint-top scorer in Derby's first season back in the top division. He left to be manager at Portsmouth in 1988 but returned to Derby as manager in 2002 in a team destined for relegation.

The board of directors between 1984 and 1986 before Robert Maxwell became chairman. Left to right: Geoff Glossop, Bill Hart (seated), Chris Charlton, Trevor East, Stuart Webb, Ian Maxwell, Brian Fearn, John Kirkland (seated) and Colin McKerrow, Fred Fern.

Ted McMinn about to unleash an unstoppable, last-minute shot to score in a 2-1 defeat against Manchester United on 10 February 1988. McMinn was signed from Sevilla and made his home debut in this match. His benefit game against Rangers in May 2006 drew in a crowd of 33,475, the current record attendance at Pride Park.

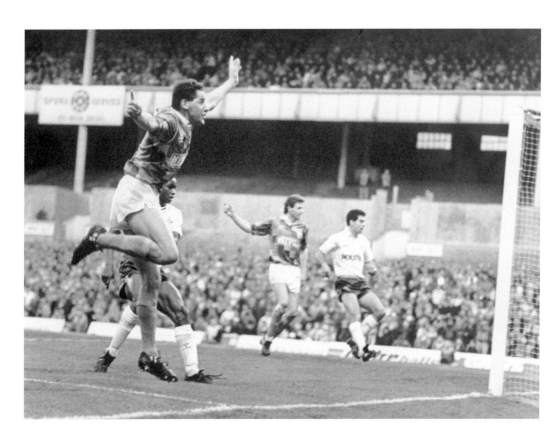

Above: McMinn scores one of his two goals against Tottenham Hotspur on 5 November 1988 in a 3-1 victory. In the same fixture a year later, he sustained a serious knee injury following a tackle by Pat van den Hauwe that put him out for a whole season. The team on that day were: Shilton, Sage, Forsyth, Cross, Wright, Blades, McMinn, Saunders, Goddard, Hebberd, Callaghan. (Courtesy of *Derby Evening Telegraph* and www.picturethepast.org.uk)

Left: Gordon Guthrie was a reserve-team player when injury forced him to quit playing and join the backroom staff. He has been with the club for several decades as a trainer and physio and can still be found on the bench at each game as kitman. He was granted a testimonial against Aston Villa in August 1987.

Frank Stapleton scored his only goal for Derby in a 2-0 victory against Southampton when on loan from Ajax in 1988. A looping header from a Nigel Callaghan cross evaded goalkeeper John Burridge and helped Derby to stay in the First Division on their first year back in the top flight. (Courtesy of *Derby Evening Telegraph* and www.picturethepast.org.uk)

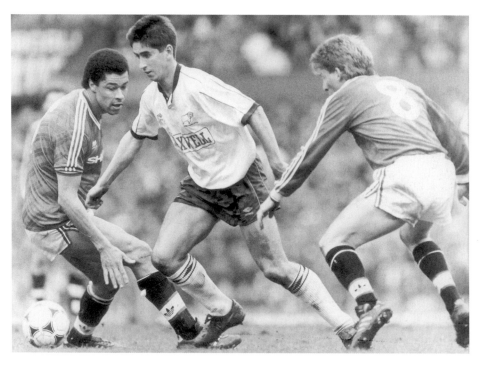

Nigel Callaghan knocking the ball past Paul McGrath (who later played for the Rams) and Gordon Strachan against Manchester United on 2 April 1988. The match ended in a 4-1 defeat for the Rams. Callaghan signed from Watford in early 1987 and returned briefly in 1990, making exactly 100 appearances for the club.

Above, left: Peter Shilton arrived from Southampton with Mark Wright for the start of the 1987/88 season and was still England's number one goalkeeper. A lack of investment after finishing fifth the previous season eventually lead to relegation and he took the option to move into management at Plymouth during the 1991/92 season, leaving his long-term understudy Martin Taylor to take over between the Derby sticks.

Above, right: Rob Hindmarch seen lifting the Derbyshire Centenary Cup in August 1988. This competition was introduced to mark the centenary of the Derbyshire Football Association and usually played between Derby County and Chesterfield. The Rams won all but one of these encounters, which were generally a pre-season affair. Rob unfortunately died in late 2002. (Courtesy of *Derby Evening Telegraph* and www.picturethepast.org.uk)

Left: Dean Saunders became Derby's first million-pound player, signing from Oxford United in October 1988. Saunders scored twice on his debut against Wimbledon. He developed a good partnership with Paul Goddard that saw Derby finish fifth in the First Division. Liverpool paid a record £2.9 million fee for him when Derby were relegated in 1991.

Mark Wright leaps highest to score the winner at Newcastle United on 2 January 1989. This was Wright's first goal for Derby since his summer move from Southampton. (Courtesy of *Derby Evening Telegraph* and www.picturethepast.org.uk)

Peter Shilton receives a special award from Stuart Webb on behalf of the club at the annual awards evening in 1990. Shilton was recognised for passing Bobby Moore's record as England's most-capped player in the run-up to the 1990 World Cup finals.

Mark Wright and Peter Shilton, who represented England during Italia '90, being presented with commemorative pieces by the Mayor of Derby. Both men were key players in helping England reach the semi-final.

Above left: Arthur Cox spent nine years as manager at Derby before having to resign due to a back injury. He joined at the start of the centenary season and, during his reign, achieved two promotions and a Wembley appearance in the Anglo-Italian Cup. There was also a top-five finish in the First Division to celebrate.

Above right: Gary Micklewhite was signed from QPR in February 1985 and, in making 112 consecutive league appearances, his consistent displays were integral to successive promotions. Bad injuries left him on the sidelines for long periods and he never really fully recovered. In all he made 288 appearances and scored 43 goals before moving into coaching in the lower leagues. He made a return in a Derby shirt in the Ted McMinn benefit game of 2006.

Ted McMinn skips over a challenge from Roy Keane in a league match against Nottingham Forest at the City Ground in April 1991. McMinn's awkward style and skill made him a target for some of the tough-tackling full-backs, especially Forest's Stuart Pearce.

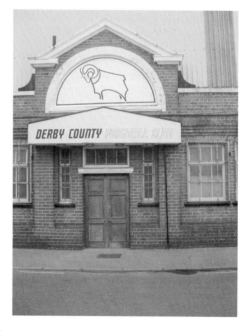

Above, left: John Harkes was a USA international player who made his name in this country with Sheffield Wednesday. He played in Derby's 1993/94 play-off final, and won 11 international caps while at Derby but was sold to the USA Soccer Federation after a few games of the promotion season of 1995/96. He played in 85 games and scored 3 goals for the Rams.

Above, right: Few people realise that the pitch level at the Baseball Ground was a number of feet below the actual street level and this accounts for the heavy pitches that were seen there during the 1960s and 1970s as surface water was unable to drain away. This photograph depicts the director's entrance at the Baseball Ground.

Since the building of the Ley Stand in 1969 little had changed at the Baseball Ground. The only perceptible alterations were that the middle tiers at either end of the stadium had been converted to seats and an executive box complex had been constructed at the corner of the Ley and Normanton Stands. Leys' works had long since been demolished and replaced by smaller industrial units. This picture of the area dates from 1992. (Courtesy of *Derby Evening Telegraph* and www.picturethepast.org.uk)

The Derby County squad for the 1992/93 season. Back row, left to right: McFarland (assistant-manager), Stallard, McMinn, Forsyth, Comyn, Sutton, Coleman, Philips, Taylor, Wassall, Nicholson, Williams, Kavanagh, Guthrie (trainer). Front row: Simpson, Micklewhite, Ramage, Gabbiadini, Kitson, Cox (manager), Pembridge, Johnson, Haywood, Round, Chalk. Note Simpson's odd shirt.

Right: The dejected Martin Taylor leaves the Wembley pitch after the 3-1 defeat to Cremonese in the Anglo-Italian Cup final of 1992/93. Taylor, a long-term understudy to Peter Shilton, had his career shattered by a badly broken leg sustained in a game at Southend United in October 1994; he had to wait until March 1996 for his next first-team appearance. (Courtesy of *Derby Evening Telegraph* and www.picturethepast.org.uk)

Below: Tommy Johnson and Darren Wassall model the home and away kits from the 1993 season. The home shirt was designed to look like a more traditional baseball shirt, while the away shirt was a series of random blue-and-black vertical, irregular stripes.

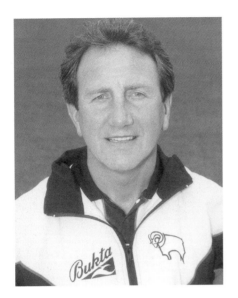

Above, left: Roy McFarland was signed by Brian Clough in August 1967 at the age of nineteen. He was involved with all of the major trophy wins, including scoring in the Charity Shield, and was selected on 28 occasions for England. After fourteen years he became manager at Bradford City but rejoined Derby as assistant-manager in late 1982 under Peter Taylor and then Arthur Cox. He had a spell as the Rams' manager from 1993–95.

Above, right: Gordon Cowans scored one of the goals that defeated Millwall in the play-off semi-finals best-remembered for the pitch invasions that marred Derby's 3-1 win in London. A Tommy Johnson goal at Wembley was not enough as Leicester won 2-1.

The old Baseball Ground, looking towards the Osmaston End. By August 1997, Derby were playing at their new 33,000-plus capacity Pride Park stadium.

The Ley Stand, which would later bear the name of two sponsors, the Co-op and Toyota. Seats were installed on the Popular Terrace in 1995; this made the stadium all-seater to comply with the Taylor Report. In one move a stadium that had regularly attracted crowds of over 40,000 was now restricted to just 18,000.

Opposite, bottom: The 1994/95 campaign was played under Roy McFarland's stewardship but his contract was not renewed at the end of the season having missed out on promotion. He left to take up the managerial position at Bolton Wanderers. Back row, left to right: Kavanagh, Wassall, Forsyth, Short, Williams, Nicholson, Kuhl. Middle row: McEwan, Durban, Hayward, Stallard, Taylor, Sutton, Johnson, Harkes, Charles, Guthrie. Front row: Sturridge, Simpson, Gabbiadini, McFarland, Cowans, Kitson, Pembridge.

Left: Chairman Lionel Pickering, whose personal wealth funded many million-pound transfer, appointed Jim Smith arrived in the summer of 1995 and had to rebuild the team after many players left during the previous close season. The appointment of McClaren as assistant-manager and the capture of van der Laan, from Port Vale, and Igor Stimac, from Hajduk Split, led to promotion to the Premier League at his first attempt.

Below: Marco Gabbiadini joined the Rams for £1m following an unsuccessful stint at Crystal Palace. He scored on his debut in a win at Portsmouth; in total he scored 68 goals in 227 games. Gabbiadini proved to be of insufficient quality in the Premier League and was eventually replaced by Ashley Ward.

Ashley Ward shoots for goal against Birmingham City on 20 April 1996. Ward's Derby career started slowly due to suffering with a persistent injury. Once fit he scored nine goals in Derby's first season in the Premier League and was the last Derby player to score at the Baseball Ground.

Dean Sturridge, about to score Derby's first goal against Crystal Palace after a through ball from Paul Simpson on 28 April 1996. A later header from Robbie van der Laan put Derby into the Premiership for the first time. Derby's team was: Hoult, Rowett, Powell, Trollope, Carbon, Stimac, van der Laan, Sturridge, Simpson, Gabbiadini and Flynn (subs Willems, Ward).

The oldest part of the Baseball Ground was the ABC Stand. With three wooden stands, change was inevitable and despite advanced plans for a redevelopment on the existing site, the opportunity to move to a purpose-built modern arena at Pride Park was too good for the Rams to turn down.

If you are interested in purchasing other books published by The History Press
or in case you have difficulty finding any History Press books in your local bookshop,
you can also place orders directly through our website

www.thehistorypress.co.uk